Nvidia: The Success Story

Full Details of their emergence as
US Second Largest Company and
effects on the Stock Market

By

Barbs Walters

Table of Contents

Introduction to Artificial Intelligence and Nvidia

Artificial Intelligence (AI) is a concept that has fascinated people for decades. It involves creating machines, computers, or software that can perform tasks that typically require human intelligence. Imagine a robot that can recognize faces, understand voice commands, or even learn from experiences. These machines are designed to perform complex tasks, such as problem-solving, learning, reasoning, and adapting to new situations, all of which were traditionally performed by humans.

What is Artificial Intelligence (AI)?

AI can be broken down into different types, based on how advanced the technology is. Some AI systems are very simple, performing repetitive tasks based on programmed rules. Others are more sophisticated, utilizing machine learning or deep learning techniques to analyze vast amounts of data and adapt to new patterns. Machine learning, a subset of AI, involves algorithms and mathematical models that allow machines to learn and improve from experience, rather than through explicit programming. Deep learning, another type of machine learning, utilizes neural networks, which are layers of artificial neurons, to process information in a way similar to the human brain.

The Rise of Nvidia in the AI Landscape

Nvidia, a leading technology company, has played a significant role in the AI landscape. Founded in 1993, Nvidia was initially known for producing computer chips that were optimized for gaming and graphic design. Over time, they expanded their focus and began to incorporate advanced technologies into their chips to assist with AI-related tasks, such as machine learning.

Nvidia chips have become powerful tools in the world of AI. These chips can process enormous amounts of data quickly and efficiently, making them ideal for training AI models, recognizing patterns, and processing complex tasks. Today, Nvidia's GPUs (Graphics Processing Units) are widely used in machine learning research, data analysis, and training AI models. They've become a cornerstone in the AI industry, and their chips have powered many of the advancements we see in machine learning applications today.

Brief History of Nvidia

Nvidia was founded in 1993 by Jensen Huang, Chris Malachowsky, and Curtis Priem, with a vision to create advanced graphics technology. In its early days, Nvidia focused on producing advanced graphics chips for the gaming industry. These chips quickly became popular for their ability to deliver high-quality graphics in computer games, leading to widespread adoption in the gaming market.

Over time, Nvidia began to explore new applications for its powerful chips. As the field of artificial intelligence began to emerge, Nvidia recognized the potential to leverage its technology in new and innovative ways. The company started to incorporate advanced features into its graphics chips to assist with AI and machine learning tasks. This move was instrumental in propelling Nvidia into the forefront of the AI landscape.

Nvidia's commitment to innovation and advanced technology has enabled them to adapt to changing market needs. Their chips' efficiency and processing power have become key components in training AI models, making them indispensable in AI research and application.

In recent years, Nvidia has seen substantial growth and success, partly driven by the growing interest in artificial intelligence technologies. Their strategic focus on AI and machine learning has played a crucial role in their rise to prominence in the technology sector.

Chapter 1:
Understanding Nvidia's
Role in AI

The Evolution of Nvidia's Products

Nvidia is a technology company that has played a significant role in shaping modern computing and artificial intelligence (AI). Founded in 1993, Nvidia started with a focus on producing graphics processing units (GPUs), which are specialized chips designed to handle complex visual processing tasks. These early GPUs were primarily used in gaming, where high-quality graphics and smooth performance were paramount.

Over time, Nvidia expanded its product line to include more advanced GPUs, catering to professional graphics applications such as animation, visual effects, and computer-aided design (CAD). These powerful GPUs became instrumental in enabling detailed graphics and computationally intensive workloads that required high-speed processing.

As technology continued to advance, Nvidia recognized the growing importance of artificial intelligence in various fields, including data analysis, machine learning, and deep learning. Nvidia's GPUs, known for their parallel processing capabilities, proved to be ideal for the massive computations required in AI workloads. Instead of using traditional central processing units (CPUs) for tasks like training AI models, researchers and developers found that Nvidia's GPUs could perform tasks more efficiently and at a larger scale.

How Nvidia Changed the Gaming Industry

Nvidia's entry into the gaming market brought a revolution in visual graphics quality. Their GPUs provided a significant improvement in the ability to render realistic and immersive environments in video games. The demand for high-quality graphics in gaming quickly grew, and Nvidia became a leader in the gaming market.

Nvidia's advanced graphics chips allowed game developers to create more intricate and detailed virtual worlds. The company's GPUs provided enhanced performance, smooth frame rates, and realistic lighting and shading effects, transforming the gaming experience. As a result, video games on Nvidia-powered systems became more immersive, drawing in millions of gamers worldwide.

With Nvidia's innovations, gaming technology continued to advance rapidly. Not only did gamers benefit from improved graphics and visual experiences, but the gaming industry as a whole saw growth, and new gaming technologies emerged. Nvidia's contributions helped shape the modern gaming landscape and continue to influence the gaming experience today.

The Transformation into AI Technology

As AI became more prominent in research and industry, Nvidia recognized the potential for its GPUs in supporting AI workloads. Unlike CPUs, which are designed for sequential processing, GPUs excelled in parallel processing tasks. This made Nvidia's GPUs highly suitable for tasks such as training complex machine learning models, which involve processing vast amounts of data simultaneously.

Nvidia's engineers and scientists began to design and optimize their GPUs specifically for AI workloads. These specialized GPUs allowed researchers to train AI models more quickly and efficiently, contributing to the rapid growth and development of machine learning and deep learning technologies.

Nvidia's GPUs have become a cornerstone in the AI industry. They provide the processing power needed to handle tasks like training neural networks, analyzing complex datasets, and performing real-time machine learning computations. As AI applications have grown in scope and sophistication, Nvidia's GPUs have proven to be essential tools in accelerating the development and deployment of AI technologies.

In addition to their hardware innovations, Nvidia also developed software tools and libraries to facilitate the use of its GPUs in AI applications. These tools have made it easier for researchers and developers to leverage Nvidia's hardware for various AI projects, further solidifying Nvidia's position as a leader in the AI industry.

Nvidia's journey from gaming graphics to AI technology illustrates the company's ability to adapt and innovate in response to changing industry demands. By leveraging the unique capabilities of its GPUs, Nvidia has significantly contributed to the advancement of AI research and application. Their expertise in hardware design and software development has made Nvidia a go-to choice for those working in the AI field, ensuring the company's continued influence in shaping the future of technology.

Chapter 2: Nvidia's Role in the AI Revolution

The Dawn of the AI Industrial Revolution

The AI Industrial Revolution is a term used to describe the rapid growth and widespread adoption of artificial intelligence technologies in various sectors of society. It signifies a transformative period where AI-powered applications are reshaping industries, businesses, and daily life. The AI Industrial Revolution is not just about creating smarter machines or computers; it's about how these advancements impact our world and drive innovation.

Nvidia has played a pivotal role in this revolution by contributing to the advancement of AI technologies. Their powerful graphics processing units (GPUs) have become essential tools for processing complex computations required in training and deploying machine learning models. The AI Industrial Revolution has accelerated due to Nvidia's GPUs, enabling faster and more efficient processing of large datasets, complex algorithms, and deep learning models.

Key Innovations in Nvidia's AI Technology

Nvidia's journey in the AI field began with optimizing its GPUs for AI workloads. One of the key innovations is the creation of specialized hardware and software tools that have greatly enhanced the performance and efficiency of AI computations. Their GPUs can process massive amounts of data simultaneously, allowing for faster training of machine learning models, reducing the time required to analyze complex datasets, and enabling real-time machine learning predictions.

Another key innovation is the development of the CUDA (Compute Unified Device Architecture) programming model. CUDA allows developers to write software that can take advantage of the parallel processing capabilities of Nvidia's GPUs. This programming model has empowered researchers and engineers to create AI algorithms and models that can leverage the full potential of Nvidia's hardware, enhancing the overall performance and accuracy of machine learning applications.

Nvidia's integration of deep learning frameworks, such as TensorFlow and PyTorch, has also been instrumental in advancing AI technologies. These frameworks, when paired with Nvidia's GPUs, provide a powerful combination that facilitates the training and deployment of sophisticated machine learning models. With the help of these tools, researchers and developers can experiment and iterate on their AI models more rapidly, accelerating the progress of AI research and application.

How Nvidia Contributes to AI Research

Nvidia's contribution to AI research extends beyond just producing hardware and software tools. The company has actively collaborated with researchers, academic institutions, and industry partners to promote innovation and knowledge-sharing in the field of artificial intelligence. Nvidia's technology and expertise have become vital assets in academic settings, where they are used to teach and train the next generation of AI experts.

Nvidia has also invested in various AI research initiatives, including partnerships and collaborations with leading AI labs around the world. These partnerships have fostered the exchange of ideas and the development of cutting-edge AI technologies. Nvidia's support has not only accelerated the pace of AI research but has also contributed to the growth and establishment of AI as a key discipline in technology and scientific research.

Moreover, Nvidia's support for hackathons, coding competitions, and AI challenges has encouraged developers and researchers to push the boundaries of AI innovation. These events provide opportunities for the community to collaborate, share insights, and showcase their advancements in the field of AI.

Nvidia's role in the AI revolution has been multi-faceted. Their innovations in hardware and software tools have made them a leader in the AI landscape, contributing to the advancement of the industry. Additionally, their collaborations and support for AI research initiatives have strengthened the growth of AI technologies in academic and industry settings.

Chapter 3: Nvidia's Market Growth

Nvidia's Surge in Market Value

Nvidia, a leading technology company known for its graphics processing units (GPUs) and AI advancements, has experienced an extraordinary surge in market value. From its beginnings in 1993, Nvidia has grown into a major player in the technology sector. Recently, the company's market value has surpassed $3 trillion, making it one of the most valuable companies in the world.

This surge in market value reflects Nvidia's strategic focus on AI and machine learning, which are driving forces behind modern technological advancements. The company's GPUs are now integral to numerous industries, from gaming to data centers, scientific research, and autonomous vehicles. Nvidia's products have become essential for the rapid processing of large datasets and complex computations, critical components in AI development.

The growing demand for AI technologies has played a significant role in Nvidia's market growth. Investors have recognized Nvidia's potential as a key player in the AI revolution, leading to increased interest and investment in the company's stock. This confidence is reflected in the rapid increase in Nvidia's share price, which has seen substantial growth over the past few years.

Factors Behind Nvidia's Increasing Market Share

Several factors have contributed to Nvidia's increasing market share and dominance in the technology sector. These include technological innovation, strategic partnerships, and expanding market applications.

1. Technological Innovation: Nvidia's commitment to innovation has been a driving force behind its market growth. The company continually develops cutting-edge GPUs that push the boundaries of performance and efficiency. Their GPUs are designed to handle intensive tasks such as AI model training, deep learning, and high-performance computing. This focus on innovation ensures

that Nvidia remains at the forefront of technological advancements, attracting a broad customer base.

2. Expanding Applications: Nvidia's GPUs are used in a wide range of applications beyond gaming. In data centers, Nvidia's GPUs accelerate data processing and analysis, making them indispensable for businesses that rely on big data and machine learning. In healthcare, Nvidia's technology helps in medical imaging and drug discovery. In the automotive industry, Nvidia's GPUs power the AI systems in autonomous vehicles. This diversification into various sectors has expanded Nvidia's market reach and increased its relevance across multiple industries.

3. Strategic Partnerships and Acquisitions: Nvidia has formed strategic partnerships with leading companies and research institutions, enhancing its market position. These collaborations have led to the integration of Nvidia's technology into various products and services, further expanding its market share. Additionally, Nvidia has made strategic acquisitions, such as the purchase of Mellanox Technologies, which strengthened its capabilities in high-performance computing and data center solutions.

4. Strong Financial Performance: Nvidia's robust financial performance has also contributed to its market growth. The company has consistently reported strong revenue growth, driven by increasing sales of its GPUs and data center products. This

financial stability and growth have instilled confidence among investors, contributing to the rise in Nvidia's stock price and market value.

5. Focus on AI and Machine Learning: Nvidia's early recognition of the potential of AI and machine learning positioned the company as a leader in these fields. Their GPUs are now the go-to choice for AI researchers and developers. Nvidia's continuous focus on enhancing AI capabilities has kept it ahead of competitors and solidified its role in the AI industry.

Nvidia's Stock Split and Impact

In an effort to make its stock more accessible to a broader range of investors, Nvidia announced a stock split. A stock split increases the number of shares in a company by issuing more shares to existing shareholders, thus reducing the price of each share while maintaining the overall value of the company. Nvidia's recent stock split increased the number of shares by a factor of ten, which effectively made the shares more affordable for smaller investors.

The stock split had several impacts:

1. Increased Accessibility: By lowering the price per share, Nvidia made its stock more accessible to individual investors and smaller investment funds. This accessibility can lead to a broader investor base and increased demand for the stock.

2. Market Sentiment: Stock splits are often perceived positively by the market, as they indicate the company's confidence in its future growth. This positive sentiment can attract more investors and further drive up the stock price.

3. Liquidity: The increased number of shares enhances the stock's liquidity, making it easier for investors to buy and sell Nvidia's stock without significantly impacting the price. Higher liquidity is generally attractive to investors, as it reduces the risk of price manipulation and makes the stock more stable.

4. Broader Ownership: The stock split allowed a more diverse group of investors to own a part of Nvidia. Broader ownership can lead to more stable long-term growth, as the

company is less reliant on large institutional investors and has a more varied shareholder base.

The decision to implement a stock split reflects Nvidia's strategic foresight in maintaining its attractiveness to investors and ensuring continued growth in market value. By making its shares more affordable, Nvidia has opened the door to a wider pool of investors, potentially driving up demand and further increasing its market value.

Chapter 4: Competition and Challenges

Apple's AI Strategy and Market Influence

Apple, a tech giant known for its innovative products and strong market presence, has a significant influence in the AI sector. While Nvidia has made a name for itself with powerful GPUs and AI-focused technologies, Apple has taken a different approach to AI, integrating it seamlessly into its ecosystem of devices and services.

Apple's AI strategy revolves around enhancing user experience through intelligent features and seamless integration. Some of the key areas where Apple leverages AI include:

1. Siri and Voice Recognition: Siri, Apple's voice assistant, uses AI to understand and respond to user commands. Siri has become more accurate and capable over the years, thanks to advances in natural language processing and machine learning.

2. Facial Recognition: Apple's Face ID technology uses AI to recognize users' faces, adding a layer of security to their devices. This technology is powered by neural networks that process and identify facial features with high accuracy.

3. Photography and Image Processing: The cameras in Apple's devices use AI to enhance photo quality. Features like Smart HDR and Night Mode rely on AI to adjust lighting, color, and clarity, ensuring that users get the best possible photos in various conditions.

4. Health and Fitness: Apple's Health app and Apple Watch use AI to track and analyze health data. These insights help users monitor their fitness levels, sleep patterns, and overall well-being.

Apple's approach to AI emphasizes privacy and user control. The company processes much of the AI data on-device rather than in the cloud, which helps protect user privacy. This strategy has resonated well with consumers who are increasingly concerned about data security.

Despite not being as vocal about AI as Nvidia, Apple's integration of AI into its products has significantly influenced the market. By focusing on enhancing user experience and privacy, Apple has set a high standard for how AI should be implemented in consumer technology.

The Role of Other AI Leaders

Besides Nvidia and Apple, several other companies are pivotal in the AI industry. These companies contribute to the advancement of AI technology and play a crucial role in shaping the future of AI. Some of the notable AI leaders include:

1. Google: Google has been a major player in AI with its deep learning research and development. The company's AI capabilities are integrated into many of its products, such as Google Assistant, Google Photos, and Google Search. Google's TensorFlow, an open-source deep learning framework, is widely used by researchers and developers to build and train machine learning models.

2. Microsoft: Microsoft has invested heavily in AI, particularly through its Azure cloud platform, which offers AI and machine learning services. Microsoft's collaboration with OpenAI has led to the development of advanced AI models, including the integration of AI capabilities into Microsoft's Office suite and other products.

3. Amazon: Amazon uses AI to power its vast e-commerce platform, recommendation systems, and Alexa voice assistant. Amazon Web Services (AWS) provides a range of AI and machine learning tools and services that enable businesses to incorporate AI into their operations.

4. IBM: IBM's Watson AI platform is known for its advanced natural language processing and data analysis capabilities. Watson has been applied in various industries, including healthcare, finance, and customer service, to provide intelligent solutions.

5. Facebook (Meta): Facebook uses AI to enhance user experience, content moderation, and targeted advertising. The company's AI research lab, FAIR (Facebook

AI Research), focuses on advancing the field of AI through cutting-edge research.

These companies, along with Nvidia and Apple, are driving innovation in AI. Their contributions are not limited to their products but extend to research, open-source tools, and industry collaborations that benefit the broader AI community.

Challenges in the AI Industry

While the AI industry is rapidly advancing, it faces several significant challenges. Addressing these challenges is crucial for the sustainable growth and ethical deployment of AI technologies.

1. Data Privacy and Security: As AI systems rely on large amounts of data, ensuring the privacy and security of this data is a major concern. Companies must navigate complex regulations and implement robust security measures to protect user data. Data breaches and misuse of personal information can lead to loss of trust and legal consequences.

2. Bias and Fairness: AI systems can inadvertently perpetuate biases present in the training data, leading to unfair or discriminatory outcomes. Ensuring fairness and eliminating bias in AI models is a significant challenge. This requires diverse training data, transparent algorithms, and continuous monitoring to detect and mitigate biases.

3. Ethical Considerations: The ethical implications of AI are vast, ranging from job displacement due to automation to the potential misuse of AI for malicious purposes. Developing ethical guidelines and ensuring responsible AI development and deployment are critical to addressing these concerns.

4. Regulation and Compliance: Governments and regulatory bodies are increasingly focusing on AI to ensure it is used responsibly. Companies must stay abreast of changing regulations and ensure compliance, which can be complex and resource-intensive. Striking a balance between innovation and regulation is essential.

5. Talent Shortage: The demand for AI talent far exceeds the supply, leading to a

competitive job market. Companies must invest in training and development to build a skilled workforce capable of advancing AI technologies. Collaborations with academic institutions and investments in education can help bridge the talent gap.

6. Technical Challenges: Developing robust and scalable AI systems involves overcoming significant technical hurdles. This includes improving the accuracy and reliability of AI models, optimizing performance for real-time applications, and ensuring the scalability of AI systems to handle large datasets and complex computations.

7. Interoperability: Ensuring that different AI systems and platforms can work together seamlessly is a challenge. Interoperability is crucial for the widespread adoption of AI

technologies across various sectors. Standardizing protocols and fostering collaboration between companies can help address this issue.

8. Environmental Impact: The computational power required for training AI models can have a significant environmental impact due to energy consumption. Developing more energy-efficient algorithms and leveraging renewable energy sources can help mitigate the environmental footprint of AI.

Chapter 5: The Future of Nvidia in AI

Emerging Trends in AI Technology

The future of artificial intelligence (AI) is shaped by several emerging trends that promise to transform various sectors. As a leader in AI hardware and software, Nvidia is poised to play a critical role in these developments. Understanding these trends helps to grasp the direction in which AI technology is heading and Nvidia's potential impact.

1. Edge Computing and AI: Edge computing involves processing data closer to its source rather than relying on centralized data centers. This trend is essential for real-time applications like autonomous vehicles, industrial automation, and smart cities. Nvidia's GPUs are increasingly being integrated into edge devices to handle AI tasks locally, enabling faster decision-making and reducing latency.

2. AI and 5G Integration: The rollout of 5G networks enhances connectivity and data transfer speeds, creating new opportunities for AI applications. With 5G, devices can communicate more efficiently, supporting AI-driven innovations in areas like telemedicine, remote work, and Internet of Things (IoT) devices. Nvidia's technology will be crucial in

leveraging 5G to develop these advanced AI solutions.

3. AI in Healthcare: AI's potential in healthcare is vast, from diagnostic tools to personalized medicine. Nvidia's GPUs power many healthcare AI applications, such as analyzing medical images, predicting patient outcomes, and drug discovery. The trend towards using AI for early detection of diseases and treatment optimization is expected to grow, with Nvidia continuing to support these advancements.

4. AI for Climate Change and Sustainability: AI can play a significant role in addressing environmental challenges. Nvidia is involved in projects that use AI to model climate patterns, optimize energy usage, and reduce carbon footprints. The future will see

increased emphasis on AI-driven sustainability initiatives, where Nvidia's technology will be key.

5. Natural Language Processing (NLP): NLP is evolving rapidly, enabling machines to understand and interact with human language more effectively. Nvidia's GPUs are essential for training complex NLP models, which are used in applications like virtual assistants, translation services, and sentiment analysis. This trend will continue to expand, with Nvidia at the forefront.

6. AI Ethics and Governance: As AI becomes more pervasive, there is a growing need for ethical guidelines and governance frameworks. Nvidia is likely to be involved in developing and adhering to these standards,

ensuring that AI technologies are used responsibly and transparently.

Nvidia's Future Projects and Plans

Nvidia's roadmap for the future includes several ambitious projects and strategic plans aimed at maintaining its leadership in AI technology. These initiatives highlight Nvidia's commitment to innovation and its vision for the future of AI.

1. Expanding AI Research: Nvidia plans to continue investing heavily in AI research and development. This includes collaborating with academic institutions, research labs, and industry partners to push the boundaries of AI technology. By fostering innovation and

supporting cutting-edge research, Nvidia aims to stay at the forefront of AI advancements.

2. AI-Powered Data Centers: Nvidia is working on creating more powerful and efficient AI data centers. These data centers will utilize advanced GPUs and AI software to handle vast amounts of data and complex computations. This initiative will support various industries that rely on big data and machine learning, from finance to scientific research.

3. Autonomous Vehicles: Nvidia is deeply involved in the development of autonomous vehicle technology. The company's DRIVE platform provides the hardware and software needed for self-driving cars to process data from sensors, make decisions, and navigate

safely. Nvidia's future plans include advancing this technology to make autonomous vehicles more reliable and widely adopted.

4. AI in Robotics: Nvidia is exploring the integration of AI into robotics, aiming to enhance the capabilities of robots in various fields, including manufacturing, healthcare, and logistics. By providing the necessary AI infrastructure, Nvidia is helping to create smarter, more efficient robots that can perform complex tasks autonomously.

5. Healthcare AI Solutions: Nvidia is focused on expanding its healthcare AI solutions. This includes developing tools for medical imaging, predictive analytics, and personalized medicine. Nvidia's Clara platform, for example, provides healthcare

professionals with AI-powered tools to improve patient care and outcomes.

6. AI for Creative Industries: Nvidia is also targeting creative industries with its AI technologies. This includes tools for content creation, such as video editing, animation, and game development. Nvidia's Omniverse platform is designed to enable real-time collaboration and simulation for artists, designers, and developers, enhancing creativity and productivity.

How AI Will Continue to Shape the Business World

AI is set to continue its transformative impact on the business world, driving innovation, efficiency, and competitive advantage across various sectors. Nvidia's contributions to AI will play a significant role in this ongoing transformation.

1. Automation and Productivity: AI enables businesses to automate repetitive and time-consuming tasks, leading to increased productivity. Nvidia's GPUs provide the processing power needed for automation technologies, from robotic process automation (RPA) to AI-driven customer service solutions. As businesses continue to adopt AI, they will become more efficient and able to focus on higher-value activities.

2. Data-Driven Decision Making: AI helps businesses make more informed decisions by analyzing large volumes of data and providing actionable insights. Nvidia's AI tools and GPUs are essential for processing

big data and extracting meaningful patterns and trends. This capability allows businesses to optimize operations, forecast demand, and improve strategic planning.

3. Customer Experience: AI enhances customer experience by providing personalized interactions and services. Nvidia's technology supports AI applications like chatbots, recommendation engines, and sentiment analysis, enabling businesses to better understand and meet customer needs. Improved customer experience can lead to increased loyalty and revenue.

4. Innovation and New Business Models: AI opens up new opportunities for innovation and the creation of novel business models. Nvidia's AI solutions enable companies to develop new products and services, enter new

markets, and disrupt traditional industries. For example, AI-powered predictive maintenance can transform manufacturing, while AI-driven financial analysis can revolutionize the finance sector.

5. Supply Chain Optimization: AI helps businesses optimize their supply chains by predicting demand, managing inventory, and reducing operational inefficiencies. Nvidia's GPUs power AI models that analyze supply chain data and identify areas for improvement. Enhanced supply chain management leads to cost savings and improved delivery times.

6. Enhanced Security: AI improves business security by detecting and responding to threats in real-time. Nvidia's AI technology is used in cybersecurity solutions that monitor

network activity, identify anomalies, and prevent cyberattacks. Businesses can protect their data and systems more effectively with AI-driven security measures.

7. Workforce Transformation: AI will continue to transform the workforce by augmenting human capabilities and creating new job opportunities. Nvidia's AI tools enable employees to perform their tasks more efficiently and effectively. While AI may automate certain roles, it also creates demand for new skills and professions, leading to a dynamic and evolving job market.

Chapter 6: Conclusion

Recap of Nvidia's Success in AI

Nvidia's journey in AI technology has been remarkable. From its early days as a graphics card manufacturer to becoming a leading force in AI, Nvidia has consistently demonstrated innovation and strategic vision.

1. Foundation and Growth: Founded in 1993, Nvidia initially focused on creating graphics processing units (GPUs) for gaming. These GPUs revolutionized the gaming industry by delivering high-quality graphics and improved performance. However, Nvidia's vision extended beyond gaming. Recognizing

the potential of GPUs in handling complex computations, the company began exploring their use in AI and machine learning.

2. AI Innovation: Nvidia's breakthrough came with the realization that GPUs could accelerate AI computations. Traditional central processing units (CPUs) were not efficient for the large-scale parallel processing required in AI. Nvidia's GPUs, with their ability to handle numerous simultaneous tasks, proved to be ideal for AI model training and inference. This innovation positioned Nvidia at the forefront of the AI revolution.

3. Product Development: Over the years, Nvidia developed a range of products tailored for AI applications. The CUDA programming model allowed developers to harness the

power of GPUs for AI and scientific computing. The launch of the Tesla line of GPUs, designed specifically for AI and deep learning, further cemented Nvidia's leadership in the AI space. These products became essential tools for researchers, developers, and companies aiming to leverage AI technology.

4. Strategic Partnerships and Acquisitions: Nvidia's growth in AI was also fueled by strategic partnerships and acquisitions. Collaborations with tech giants like Microsoft, Google, and Amazon enabled Nvidia to integrate its GPUs into major AI platforms and services. The acquisition of Mellanox Technologies expanded Nvidia's capabilities in high-performance computing and data centers, enhancing its AI infrastructure.

5. Market Leadership: Nvidia's success in AI translated into significant market growth. The company's market value surged, reflecting investor confidence in its AI strategy and products. Nvidia's GPUs became the industry standard for AI research and applications, used by leading companies and institutions worldwide.

The Broader Impact of Nvidia's Growth

Nvidia's rise in the AI sector has had a profound impact on various industries and the broader technology landscape. The company's innovations have enabled advancements in numerous fields, demonstrating the transformative power of AI.

1. Healthcare: Nvidia's AI technology has revolutionized healthcare. AI-powered medical imaging, diagnostic tools, and predictive analytics have improved patient outcomes and streamlined healthcare processes. For instance, AI models trained on Nvidia GPUs can detect diseases like cancer at early stages, providing timely and accurate diagnoses.

2. Autonomous Vehicles: Nvidia's contributions to the development of autonomous vehicles have been significant. The Nvidia DRIVE platform powers the AI systems in self-driving cars, enabling them to process data from sensors, make real-time decisions, and navigate safely. This

technology promises to reduce traffic accidents, enhance mobility, and transform the transportation industry.

3. Scientific Research: Researchers across various disciplines use Nvidia's AI technology to tackle complex problems. From climate modeling to genomics, Nvidia's GPUs facilitate high-performance computing and data analysis, driving breakthroughs and discoveries. The ability to process vast amounts of data quickly and accurately accelerates research and innovation.

4. Entertainment and Media: Nvidia's GPUs have transformed the entertainment industry by enabling realistic graphics, special effects, and animation. AI-driven tools enhance content creation, making it easier for artists and developers to produce high-quality

visuals and interactive experiences. This impact extends to virtual and augmented reality, where Nvidia's technology powers immersive environments.

5. Manufacturing and Industry: AI applications in manufacturing, powered by Nvidia's technology, optimize production processes, predictive maintenance, and quality control. AI models can predict equipment failures, reducing downtime and maintenance costs. This efficiency leads to higher productivity and cost savings for manufacturers.

6. Financial Services: In the financial sector, AI models run on Nvidia GPUs analyze market trends, detect fraud, and provide personalized financial advice. These capabilities enhance decision-making, risk

management, and customer service, contributing to the efficiency and security of financial operations.

Reflections and Future Considerations

As we reflect on Nvidia's journey and success in AI, it is essential to consider the future trajectory of the company and the AI industry. Several key factors will shape Nvidia's continued growth and impact.

1. Ethical AI Development: With the widespread adoption of AI, ethical considerations become increasingly important. Nvidia, as a leader in AI, has a responsibility to ensure that its technology is used responsibly and ethically. This includes

addressing issues like bias in AI models, data privacy, and the potential for AI to be used in harmful ways. Nvidia must work with policymakers, industry leaders, and researchers to develop ethical guidelines and standards.

2. Sustainability: The environmental impact of AI and high-performance computing is a growing concern. Training large AI models requires substantial energy resources. Nvidia must focus on developing energy-efficient GPUs and supporting sustainable practices in AI development. This includes exploring renewable energy sources and optimizing algorithms to reduce energy consumption.

3. Talent Development: The demand for AI talent continues to grow. Nvidia can play a crucial role in fostering the next generation of

AI professionals. This includes investing in education, providing training programs, and collaborating with academic institutions. By supporting the development of AI talent, Nvidia ensures a skilled workforce capable of advancing AI technology.

4. Innovation and Adaptability: The AI landscape is dynamic and rapidly evolving. Nvidia must continue to innovate and adapt to stay ahead. This involves not only improving existing products but also exploring new areas of AI application. Nvidia's ability to anticipate market trends and respond to technological advancements will be key to its sustained success.

5. Global Collaboration: AI development is a global effort that requires collaboration across borders. Nvidia should continue to

engage with international partners, research institutions, and governments to advance AI research and applications. Global collaboration fosters knowledge sharing, standardizes practices, and addresses global challenges through AI.

6. Community Engagement: Engaging with the AI community and end-users is essential for understanding their needs and challenges. Nvidia should maintain an open dialogue with developers, researchers, and businesses to gather feedback and insights. This engagement ensures that Nvidia's products and solutions are aligned with the needs of the AI community.

www.ingramcontent.com/pod-product-compliance
Lightning Source LLC
Chambersburg PA
CBHW070128230526
45472CB00004B/1465